MIDLOTHIAN LIBRARIES

D1390889

9013

LOTHIAN LIBRARY SE

/renew this item by the l
ive your borrower
on, online
mid

I WISH THAT I DIDN'T SOMETIMES, BUT...

...I REMEMBER EVERYTHING ABOUT THAT CURSED, UNSPEAKABLY UNHAPPY NIGHT TWELVE YEARS AGO...

NO LAST NAME.

JUST DANIEL X.

I HAVE TO TELL
YOU ONE LAST
THING ABOUT
THAT NIGHT.

I MUST GET IT
OUT.

EVEN THOUGH I WAS ONLY THREE
YEARS OLD, I AM ASHAMED THAT I DIDN'T
FIGHT THE PRAYER TO THE DEATH...

GRRRRR

YOU'RE VERY IMPRESSIVE AND SCARY, ORKNG—

MAY I CALL YOU ORKNG?

IS THAT YOUR LAST WISH?

OH, I HOPE NOT.

SAY, I'VE HEARD YOU HAVE LEVEL 4 STRENGTH.

TRUE OR FALSE?

WOW~!

THUD

AND YOU'RE A SHAPE-SHIFTER TOO?

YOU...

EXTERMI-
NATED.

TWELVE YEARS
HAVE PASSED SINCE
THAT NIGHT.

I'M
FIFTEEN
NOW.

ALL GROWN UP.
SORT OF.

SINCE MY
MOM AND DAD
DIED...

...SINCE I
BECAME
AN ALIEN
HUNTER...

...I'VE BEEN KIDNAPPED BY FACELESS METALLIC HUMANOIDS.

TWICE.

I'VE BEEN CHASED AND CAPTURED BY A SHAPE-SHIFTING PROTO-PLASM IN LONDON WHO WANTED TO MAKE ME INTO A JELLY SANDWICH, WITHOUT THE BREAD.

I'VE BEEN IN HAND-TO-ANTENNAE COMBAT WITH AN ENTIRE CIVILIZATION OF INSECTS IN MEXICO CITY, CUERNAVACA, AND ACAPULCO.

I'VE HAD MY FACE RUN OVER AGAIN AND AGAIN—FOR DAYS—BY SELF-REPLICATING MACHINES THAT WERE ABOUT TO TAKE OVER DETROIT.

A BILLION OR SO "LITTLE WAILING MOUTHS" CONNECTED THROUGH AN ELECTRICAL NETWORK TO A SINGLE MIND ATE AND DIGESTED ME IN HAMBURG, GERMANY.

THEY WERE ALL ON THIS LIST, AND NOW THEY'RE ALL GONE.

LET ME CHECK.

THE LIST—

IT CONTAINS THE NAMES, FULL DESCRIPTIONS...

...AND APPROXIMATE WHEREABOUTS OF THE KNOWN OUTLAW ALIENS CURRENTLY ROAMING THE EARTH.

AND TRUST ME ON THIS—

THEY ARE OUT THERE, WATCHING AND STUDYING US.

CREAK

COOL, LOOKS LIKE NO ONE BROKE IN.

WHO'S NEXT...?

NUMBER 6: ERGENT SETH.

HE'S BASED IN L.A., SOMEWHERE CALLED MALIBU.

HE SPECIALIZES IN GENOCIDE, AND HE'S ALREADY DEVASTATED ALPAR NOK.

NOW HE'S AFTER TERRA FIRMA— EARTH— TO DESTROY EVERY LIFE-FORM.

IT'S CRUCIAL TO STOP HIM BEFORE HE GETS ON A ROLL...

...SO THE LIST STRONGLY RECOMMENDS HIM AS THE NEXT TARGET.

DING DONG..

L.A....

TIME TO LEAVE THIS HOUSE.

HUH?

I NEVER HAVE VISITORS. WHO CAN IT BE?

SAY, SOMETHING AS SIMPLE AS A SIGN LIKE THIS?

LA

HOONK

VROOM

MY MOM AND DAD AND FRIENDS ARE EASY TOO.

I CREATE THEM A LOT, WHEN I'M AFRAID OR LONELY.

THEY'RE LIKE A RECIPE YOU'VE DONE OVER AND OVER AGAIN UNTIL YOU CAN DO IT IN YOUR SLEEP.

29

WHA ─?!

SO WHO'S CHASING WHOM?

STAB

AND WHICH OF MY MOUTHS GETS TO TAKE A HUGE BITE OUT OF YOU FIRST?

ARGH!

SO—

NUMBER 6 SOMEHOW KNOWS I'M COMING.

WHAT OTHER POWERS DOES ERGENT SETH HAVE THAT ARE AS IMPRESSIVE AS MY OWN?

COLD.

ONLY NATURAL, I GUESS.

MAYBE I SHOULD HEAT UP THE GATORADE OVER THE FIRE...

WISH I HAD A HOT MEAL.

!!

......

...COME TO THINK OF IT...

...SOME OF THE ALIEN OUTLAWS CAN SEE IN THE DARK LIKE IT'S DAYLIGHT.

WHAT IF ONE OF THEM'S LURKING OUT HERE...?!

WHY DID I STAY UP LATE WATCHING THE BLAIR WITCH PROJECT A FEW NIGHTS AGO?!

MAYBE I SHOULD HAVE TRIED HARDER TO FIND A TOWN.

I DON'T WANNA BE ALONE—!!

RUSTLE

THERE YOU ARE.

DANIEL X

HEY, WILLY.

SURVIVAL TRAINING.

I LOVE IT.

THE GREAT OUTDOORS!

THE PACIFIC NORTH-WEST! WOW!

WILLY IS AROUND MY AGE—FIFTEEN OR SO.

HE'S ALWAYS READY, WILLING, AND ABLE TO TRY ANYTHING, AND MIX IT UP WITH ANY **THING**.

YOU KNOW HOW TO TRAVEL, DANIEL.

IF ANYONE ENJOYS CHASING DOWN ALIENS AS MUCH AS I DO, IT'S WILLY.

CHEX MIX!

RIGHT-EOUS!

JOE-JOE, ON THE OTHER HAND...

...IS MORE LIKE ALL STOMACH.

HEY! THAT WAS SUPPOSED TO BE MY BREAKFAST TOMORROW!

NO WONDER IT WAS SO GOOD!

WHICH IS CRAZY, BECAUSE HE'S SUPER SKINNY.

HE'S ALSO MESSY, AN ATHLETE AT NOTHING BUT COMPETITIVE EATING, AND THE MOST SARCASTIC, FUNNIEST MOTORMOUTH I KNOW.

OH, WOW!

SPRUCE, CEDARS...

...DOUG-LAS FIRS, CYPRESS-ES.

AMAZING!

I LOVE IT HERE.

GREAT SPOT, DANIEL.

SHE'S TALL, WITH PIN-STRAIGHT BLOND HAIR THAT FLOWS LIKE A WATERFALL OF FLAME DOWN HER BACK.

SHE'S PROBABLY THE MOST BEAUTIFUL GIRL I'VE EVER SEEN—JUST MY OPINION, OF COURSE.

BUT THE NEAT PART IS THAT, HANDS DOWN, DANA'S THE MOST GENUINE PERSON I'VE MET.

NO EGO, NO BIG HEAD, NO AGENDA.

SWEET SPOT, DANIEL.

I LOVE THE COLD BY ITSELF, BUT WET TOO? AND LOUSY GRUB.

JOE'S ACTUALLY RIGHT FOR ONCE. THIS PLACE IS A DUMP.

A DUMP?!

THE PACIFIC NORTHWEST IS LIKE ONE OF THE BIOLOGICALLY RICHEST AREAS IN NORTH AMERICA.

MAYBE IN ALL THE TEMPERATE AREAS OF THE WORLD.

BESIDES ALL OF THE CONIFEROUS GROWTH...

...IT'S HOME TO THE MOURNING DOVE AND THE WESTERN FENCE LIZARD.

HEY, YOU'RE RIGHT, EMMA.

THIS ECO-BIOSYSTEM THINGY IS REALLY START-ING TO GROW ON ME. IN FACT...

WILL YOU MARRY ME?

SERI-OUSLY. I LOVE YOU, TREE.

HEY!!

ENOUGH, CLOWN BOY.

I CALL TRIVIAL PURSUIT.

FIRST QUESTION, DANA.

CATEGORY IS ENTERTAINMENT. WHO PLAYED THE ROLE OF GEORGE BAILEY IN FRANK CAPRA'S CHRISTMAS CLASSIC, *IT'S A WONDERFUL LIFE?*

I KNOW YOU KNOW IT, GIRL.

SAMUEL L. JACKSON...

...

JIMMY STEWART.

NO, WAIT. IT WAS MINI-ME!

YOU GO, GIRL.

NEXT QUESTION — JOE.

CATEGORY IS THEORETICAL PHYSICS.

IN QUANTUM ELECTRODYNAMICS, WHAT IS THE FULL SCATTERING AMPLITUDE THE SUM OF?

WHAT?!

WH-WH-WHAT?!

THEORETICAL PHYSICS! E=MC².

HOW SHOULD I KNOW? LET ME SEE THAT CARD!

INCOR-RECT.

DANIEL, YOUR TURN.

SCIENCE AND NATURE.

WHAT DOES ELEPHANT MEAN IN LATIN?

AN ELEPHANT QUESTION!

I GET THE THERMO WHATZIT AND DANIEL, THE ELEPHANT NERD, GETS AN ELE-PHANT QUESTION?

BESIDES, HE KNOWS LATIN.

AND ABOUT A HUNDRED OTHER LAN-GUAGES.

HUGE ARCH.

ELE MEANS ARCH AND PHANT MEANS HUGE.

CORRECT.

TCH!

YOU KNOW WHAT, GUYS? I THINK I'M GONNA HIT THE SACK.

I'VE HAD A LONG, HARD ONE TODAY.

YOU DO LOOK TIRED, SO GET SOME REST.

YOU GOT MY BACK TONIGHT?

ANYTHING GETS CLOSE TO THIS CAMPFIRE THAT JOE CAN'T EAT...

...YOU'RE GOING TO BE THE FIRST TO KNOW.

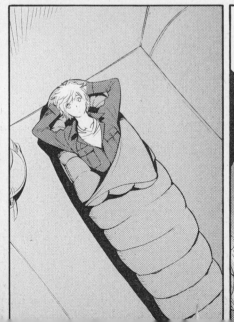

HEY, YOU. WHY ARE YOU STILL UP?

YOU SHOULD GET SOME REST.

WELL...

...WHY DO I ONLY GET TO MEET THE BAD ALIENS?

I'M PRETTY SURE THERE ARE SOME GOOD ONES OUT THERE, BUT I'VE NEVER MET ONE.

DO YOU THINK I'LL EVER GET TO MEET A GOOD ALIEN?

YOU MEET ONE EVERY DAY.

EVERY TIME YOU LOOK IN A MIRROR.

YOU MEAN ME?

YOU THINK I'M AN ALIEN TOO?

IT WOULDN'T MAKE ANY SENSE IF YOU'RE NOT.

ANYWAY, DON'T GET TOO DEEP INTO THOSE THOUGHTS AND GO TO SLEEP.

GOOD NIGHT, DANNYBOY.

ACCORDING TO THE LIST...

...ERGENT SETH, I MEAN NUMBER 6...

...LIVES SOMEWHERE CALLED MALIBU.

WE'LL BE GOING NOW...

I'M GLAD WE GOT A PLACE YOU LIKE.

NO, WAIT!

STAY AROUND FOR DINNER. I'LL COOK!

I SHOULD TRY OUT THIS GOURMET KITCHEN, RIGHT?

HA...SO THIS IS HIGH SCHOOL.

MURMUR   MURMUR

UGH.

MY SNEAKERS ARE SO SIX MONTHS AGO.

EVERY-BODY'S CHECKING OUT MY SHOES.

EVERY-BODY'S LOOKING AT ME! DON'T LOOK AT ME. PLEASE!

...

WELL, WELL. AMANDA'S DEFINITELY FLIRTING WITH ME.

I HATE THIS...

FIRST DAY'S OVER, AND I HAVEN'T EVEN TALKED TO ANYBODY.

I DON'T WANT TO DO THIS ANYMORE. I HATE THIS SCHOOL.

WHOSE THOUGHTS ARE THESE?

WOW...

GORGEOUS —!!

SO DO YOU HAVE A LAST NAME TOO, DANIEL?

ERM, HOPPER. DANIEL HOPPER.

I'M PHOEBE COOK.

NICE TO MEET YOU, DANIEL HOPPER.

I ACTUALLY COULD USE SOME HELP. JUST TO GET MY LOCKER BACK OPEN.

THUD

FRANKLY, I DON'T KNOW IF I CAN LUG ALL THESE BOOKS HOME.

YOU'RE IN LUCK. LUGGING IS ONE OF MY BETTER TALENTS.

I THOUGHT YOU WERE LOOKING FOR THE LIBRARY, DANIEL.

I GOT A BETTER OFFER, I GUESS.

I GUESS YOU DID.

WELL, LET'S SEE HOW YOU LUG.

WOW, YOU DO MOVE AROUND A LOT.

TOO MUCH.

MY FAMILY MOVES A LOT TOO.

THEY'RE KIND OF FREE SPIRITS.

DANIEL IS GORGEOUS!

I WONDER IF HE WOULD MAYBE ASK ME OUT?

...!!

SO THIS IS IT. THAT'S MY PLACE.

IT'S OKAY, DANIEL.

GO FOR IT.

EH-HEH-HEH.

AH-HA-HA.

WHY DON'T WE GO TO A MOVIE, OR MAYBE EXPLORE GLENDALE SOMETIME?

OKAY.

THE MOVIES, WHATEVER. THAT'D BE GREAT. GOOD.

YOU KNOW WHAT I MEAN.

BYE-BYE.

WERE YOU REALLY LOOKING FOR THE LIBRARY?

I WAS LOOKING FOR YOU.

NOPE.

GOOD ANSWER.

AND NO, I DIDN'T CREATE PHOEBE COOK, IN CASE YOU'RE ONE OF THOSE PEOPLE WHO LIKE TO LOOK AHEAD IN A STORY.

ALIEN: ERGENT SETH, NUMBER 6
HUMAN ALIAS(ES): ? CHANGES NAMES ON AN AS-NEEDED BASIS, OFTEN HOURLY.
AREA OF INFESTATION: L.A. AND ORANGE COUNTY, CALIFORNIA. CENTRAL CITY. EAST L.A. ARIZONA. NEVADA. MEXICO. SOUTH AND CENTRAL AMERICA. AND STILL BRANCHING OUT.
ILLEGAL ACTIVITIES: DRUG DEALING, MASS MURDER, ABDUCTIONS, TORTURE, MIND CONTROL, AND POSSESSION. DID WE MENTION MASS MURDER?

PLANET OF ORIGIN: GORTO 4.
ALIEN SPECIES: VERMGYPIAN (SEE FOOTNOTE).
CURRENT DANGER LEVEL: EXTREMELY HIGH. SETH'S GOAL IS TO DE-POPULATE EARTH, THEN COLONIZE IT WITH HIS SPECIES. THIS VIOLATES EVERY MORAL AND ETHICAL CODE EXTANT.
SPECIAL ABILITIES: TELEPATHY, EXTRATERRESTRIAL LEVEL 7 SPEED, LEVEL 7 STRENGTH, SHAPE-SHIFTING, CUNNING, GENERAL VICIOUSNESS.

SLAM SKID CRASH

...

AAARGH!

NO!

SCREECH

AAAAACK!!

MICHELLE!!

HAS ANYONE SEEN MY DAUGHTER?!

SHE'S NINE WITH BROWN HAIR AND—

SHE JUST DISAPPEARED!!

MY SON!!

MY SON DISAPPEARED TOO!

WHAT'S GOING ON?!

MY BABY!!

!!

THAT SHOULD DO FOR TODAY.

RETREAT.

YES, SIR.

THUD

!

FWSH

TSK. I WAS TOO LATE.

DANIEL X

CHAPTER 3

ALL DONE.

OH, ALREADY?

THAT WAS QUICK.

SERIOUSLY, GUYS...

...I'M NOTHING WITHOUT YOU.

AND YOU THANK US HOW...?

I WAS GONNA ORDER PIZZ—

PIZZA! I'LL ORDER!!

W-W-W-WAIT!! I CAN'T LET YOU ORDE—

NO, NOT ONE WITH EVERYTHING.

ONE OF EVERYTHING. I'D LIKE THE ENTIRE MENU.

SHHH.

HELLO?

IN FACT, MAKE IT TWO ENTIRE MENUS.

DOMINO'S?

RING

I DON'T DO PROCESSED FLOUR. HELLO? THIS IS CALIFORNIA.

THERE HAS TO BE A WHOLE FOODS AROUND HERE.

HUH?

IT SHOULD BE THE PIZZA PLACE, CONFIRMING JOE'S INSANE ORDER.

RING

GIMME.

DON'T CANCEL ANYTHING!

HELLO?

HELLO, INDEED.

!!! IT'S SETH!

...WHO'S THIS?

WHO'S THIS? NOW IS THAT REMOTELY PROPER ETIQUETTE?

WOULDN'T "MAY I HELP YOU?" BE A TAD MORE POLITE? BAD ENOUGH THEY SEND A BOY FOR ME, BUT A CRUDE AMERICAN ONE WITH NO MANNERS?

NONETHELESS, TO ANSWER YOUR IMPOLITE QUESTION, I THINK YOU KNOW WHO I AM.

THOUGH I DARESAY, IF YOU DON'T FOLLOW MY ADVICE VERY, VERY SOON...

NOTHING THAT HAS EVER ENCOUNTERED ME HAS LIVED TO TELL THE TALE—

OKAY. THAT'S INTER-ESTING.

BUT MY NAME'S NOT DANIEL, AND I HAVE NO IDEA WHAT YOU'RE TALKING ABOUT.

YOU HAVE A GOOD DAY.

bip

RING

WHAT WAS THAT?

WAS IT—

RRRRRRING

RRRRRRRING

I CAN'T FAKE IT ANYMORE.

I LIED TO YOU ABOUT MY DAD MOVING US BECAUSE OF HIS JOB. WE RELOCATED...

...BECAUSE SOMETHING AWFUL, REALLY AWFUL, HAPPENED TO OUR FAMILY.

LAST JULY, MY LITTLE SISTER, ALLISON, WENT OUT TO CHALK ON THE DRIVEWAY AFTER SWIMMING LESSONS, AND...

...SHE NEVER CAME BACK. SHE WAS ABDUCTED.

SOMEBODY TOOK HER, DANIEL.

SHE WAS SIX YEARS OLD. SHE'D BE SEVEN NOW.

I'VE BEEN TRYING TO STAY CALM...

...BUT EVER SINCE THAT INCIDENT DOWNTOWN...

...I CAN'T STOP THINKING ABOUT MY POOR SISTER...

...I'M SORRY.

THIS IS...?

THIS IS THE HOUSE I LIVED IN IN PORTLAND!

DANIEL! C'MERE, DANIEL!

WE WANT TO TALK TO YOU, BUDDY.

WHERE ARE YOUR CRAZY MOM AND DAD?

GASP

THIS CUTIE?

YOU RULE, EMMA.

I OWE YOU ONE.

I OWE YOU.

THANKS FOR THINKING ME HERE. I JUST LOVE DOGGIES.

DANIEL? IS THAT YOU?

WHAT ARE YOU DOING HERE?

SORRY. IT WAS TOO LATE TO RING THE DOORBELL. I GOT INTO A MAJOR BLOWOUT WITH MY PARENTS...

I WOULDN'T STOP HELPING IF YOU TOLD ME TO.

WE'RE GOING TO FIND YOUR SISTER. SOMEHOW.

THANK YOU...

THAT'S THE POLICE FILE ON MY SISTER'S CASE. MY FOLKS DON'T KNOW I HAVE IT.

THERE HAD BEEN NO WITNESSES.

NO SIGN OF SUSPICIOUS VEHICLES. NO NOTHING.

ALLISON HAD GONE OUT TO PLAY AT AROUND ONE IN THE AFTERNOON.

WHEN HER MOTHER CHECKED ON HER, SHE WAS SIMPLY AND INEXPLICABLY GONE. AND SHE HAS NOT BEEN HEARD FROM AGAIN.

THIS HAS SOMETHING TO DO WITH SETH.

HERE'S A LIST TOO... HOW MANY KIDS DID HE KIDNAP?

!!

LET'S TRY GOOGLING THE NAMES.

THE ONES HERE?

TAP

TAP

Potential Pattern

Awaiting GP

8907-4574

216-9543

3-5311

4355

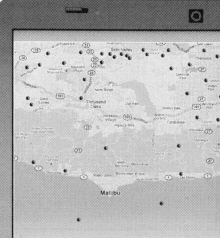

Malibu

IT'S OKAY, DANIEL. HE'S GONE.

LET ME FIX A PLACE FOR YOU TO SLEEP.

GASP

SHE ISN'T THINKING THAT I...

...I MEAN, SHE DOESN'T THINK THAT SHE AND I WOULD...

...WOULD... WHAT?

YOU SLEEP IN THE CLOSET HERE, DANIEL.

IN CASE MY MOM OR DAD OPENS THE DOOR, OKAY?

IS SHE UP
ALREADY?

NO SOUND
OF A
SHOWER.

WHERE
IS SHE?

SHE'S NOT
ANYWHERE
IN THE BED-
ROOMS.

NOT IN
THE ATTIC
EITHER.

PHOEBE'S
GONE.

DANIEL X

CHAPTER 4

WHAT DO YOU MEAN SHE'S NOT IN THE HOUSE?

I NOTICED HER SCHOOL BAG'S GONE.

PHOEBE'S PARENTS!!

MAYBE SHE WENT IN EARLY TO STUDY.

I'M SURE THERE'S A PERFECTLY REASONABLE EXPLANATION.

WHO ARE YOU CALLING?

THE POLICE.

HONEY, THERE'S NO NEED TO PANIC. WE SHOULD THINK THIS THROUGH.

SHE'S THE ONLY DAUGHTER WE HAVE LEFT.

YOU THINK IT THROUGH WHILE I DO SOMETHING.

SLAM

PHOEBE ISN'T HERE AT SCHOOL.

I DON'T WANT TO EVEN THINK ABOUT IT, BUT...

...DID SETH ALREADY...?

YOU'RE LIKE MY GUARDIAN ANGEL.

YEAH, OR MAYBE I'M THE ONE WHO LED SETH TO YOU.

PHOEBE!!

!

?!

WHAT?

!!

WHAT DO YOU THINK YOU'RE DOING?

AIEEEEEEEEE!!!!!

!!

THUD

WHAM

SO THAT PART OF THE STORY WAS TRUE.

YOU REALLY ARE OFF-LOADING KIDS FROM THE EARTH. YOU'RE NOTHING BUT A SLAVE TRADER.

MOVE, MOVE, MOVE!

C'MON, THAT'S NOT ALL I AM.

DON'T FORGET ALL THE STEALING, MURDERING, AND DRUG DEALING I DO.

NOW THAT WE'VE COME FACE-TO-FACE, SETH...

...MY ONLY REGRET IS THAT YOU'RE NOT THE INSECTLIKE LOWLIFE WHO ACTUALLY KILLED MY FOLKS.

OH, I JUST MIGHT BE THEIR KILLER AFTER ALL.

NO, YOU'RE NOT. THE CREATURE WHO TOOK OUT MY PARENTS...

...THE ONE WHO IS GOING TO PAY WITH HIS LIFE...

...IS THE PRAYER.

YOU'RE ONLY *SIXTH* ON MY LIST, SETH. DREAM ON!

ARRGH!!

ACK!

THUD

RUMBLE

I NEED TO STAY UPBEAT... THE NIGHT IS DARKEST BEFORE THE DAWN.

YEAH, RIGHT.

MAKES YOU STRONGER; CRIPPLES YOU FOREVER.

I'M A LOSER, COMPLETE AND UTTER.

I GUESS IT WAS A FAMILY TRADITION.

YOU'RE NOT A LOSER!

EVERY CLOUD HAS A SILVER LINING.

WHAT DOESN'T KILL YOU MAKES YOU STRONGER.

YOU ARE NOT A LOSER, DANIEL.

SEEMS LIKE THE BLEEDING STOPPED.

THE PAIN IS MANAGE-ABLE TOO.

HOW LONG HAS IT BEEN?

AT LEAST I CAN SIT UP...

CLICK

HERE, BOY.

OH, WHAT'S WRONG?

DOES THE LITTLE DOGGIE HAVE A TUM-TUM ACHE?

DON'T WANT TO PLAY EPIC HERO ANYMORE?

YOU'RE PATHETIC, DO YOU KNOW THAT? YOU ACTUALLY THOUGHT YOU COULD COME AFTER ME? AND WIN?

I EVEN WARNED YOU.

LOSERS LIKE YOU ARE NEVER SATISFIED UNTIL SOMEONE ACTUALLY HANDS THEM THEIR HEADS.

BUT LOSERS SUCH AS YOURSELF NEVER LEARN, I SUPPOSE.

I SHOULD HAVE LISTENED TO YOU.

PLEASE, PLEASE.

I'LL DO ANYTHING YOU WANT.

OF COURSE YOU WILL.

SLAM

...

HEY, HOW'S IT GOING?

DANIEL!

WE'RE TRYING TO FIND A LIFE-BOAT OR AN ESCAPE POD, BUT NO LUCK.

BUT YOU KNOW...

...EVEN IF WE FIND ONE, WE WON'T KNOW HOW TO OPER-ATE IT.

WE DON'T EVEN KNOW THE DIRECTION BACK TO EARTH.

THAT'S TRUE.

STILL, KEEP SEARCHING. IF NOT A WAY OUT, AT LEAST FIND A WAY TO STRIKE BACK AT SETH AND HIS GOONS.

OKAY, OKAY.

WAIT. LOOK AT THAT!

OH!

WHAT IS IT?

WILL LET YOU KNOW WHEN WE'RE SURE. TALK TO YOU LATER!

EMMA, DANA...

...WHAT ABOUT YOU GUYS?

HERE YOU GO!

IT'S A FRIENDSHIP BRACELET!

IT'LL KEEP YOU SAFE, OKAY?

HOW LONG HAVE YOU BEEN HERE?

MONTHS? YEARS?

DUNNO.

DUNNO.

WHERE ARE THE OLDER KIDS?

TAKEN AWAY.

YOU SMILED! YOU'RE MUCH CUTER WHEN YOU SMILE!

DANA...

WILLY, JOE, ANY UPDATES?

STILL NOT SURE.

I THINK IT MIGHT BE THE BRIDGE...

...BUT DON'T HOLD YOUR BREATH.

I'LL...

...NEVER UNDERESTIMATE AN OPPONENT AGAIN.

WHAT AM I THINKING?

THERE ISN'T GOING TO BE AN AGAIN.

CLICK

!

GET HIM OUT.

WHERE TO NOW?

THE EXECUTION CHAMBER?

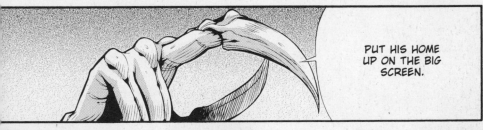

PUT HIS HOME UP ON THE BIG SCREEN.

WHY HAVE WE COME BACK?

AND WHY IS TERRA FIRMA GREENISH AT THE EDGES?

WHAT HAVE YOU DONE NOW, SETH?

ALPAR NOK?

MY HOME?

DANIEL X

TH-
THESE
RUINS...

CHAPTER 5

UNREAL, ISN'T IT?

SOMETIMES EVEN I CAN'T BELIEVE IT.

I MEAN, EVER SINCE I WAS LITTLE...

...I ALWAYS DREAMED OF COMMITTING MASS DESTRUCTION.

BUT ON THIS KIND OF SCALE?

IT'S MORE THAN EVEN I HAD A RIGHT TO EXPECT.

YOUR FELLOW ALPARIANS?

THE FEW WHO ARE STILL ALIVE SCURRY THROUGH THE RUINS LIKE RATS.

WHERE IS EVERYONE?

!!

THEY HAVE NO POWERS, NO HOPE, NO REASON TO LIVE, REALLY.

BUT STILL THEY STUMBLE ON.

PATHETIC.

PROTECTORS OF THE UNIVERSE?

GUESS THEY SHOULD HAVE WORRIED MORE ABOUT PROTECTING THEMSELVES.

......

WHAT DO YOU MEAN, "PROTECTORS OF THE UNIVERSE"?

YOU ARE CLUELESS, AREN'T YOU?

BEHOLD, ALPAR NOK, THE HOME OF THE ALIEN HUNTERS...

...THE UNIVERSE'S ANSWER TO INJUSTICE AND EVIL!

YOUR PARENTS WERE SENT TO EARTH TO PROTECT THE OH-SO-SPECIAL HUMANS FROM THE OUTER ONES...

...AS THEY LIKE TO CALL US.

BECAUSE A FEW PATHETIC ALPARIANS WERE BORN WITH SOME ABILITY TO MANIPULATE THE UNIVERSAL FORCE...

...IT WAS THOUGHT YOU COULD PROTECT THE GOOD FROM THE EVIL.

AS IF GOOD AND EVIL AREN'T JUST FAIRY TALES MADE UP FOR SMALL CHILDREN.

THERE ARE THE *STRONG* AND THEN THERE ARE THE *WEAK*.

......

173

COULD IT BE THE AIR OF MY HOME-LAND?

I COULD SHATTER THESE SHACKLES EASILY, BUT THERE'S SO MANY OF THEM.

I NEED TO DO SOMETHING BEFORE SETH FINDS OUT THAT MY ABILITIES ARE COMING BACK.

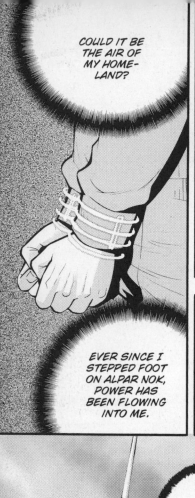

EVER SINCE I STEPPED FOOT ON ALPAR NOK, POWER HAS BEEN FLOWING INTO ME.

SOMETHING OUTRAGEOUS TO DISTRACT THEM ALL.

...WAIT A SECOND.

THAT BUILDING IS LEANING TOWARD US.

DANIEL, IT DOES LOOK VERY UNSTABLE.

WE COULD DO THIS.

JUST A KICK WOULD MAKE IT—

TAP

CREAK

!!

CREAK

!!

HEY GUYS, NOT YET!

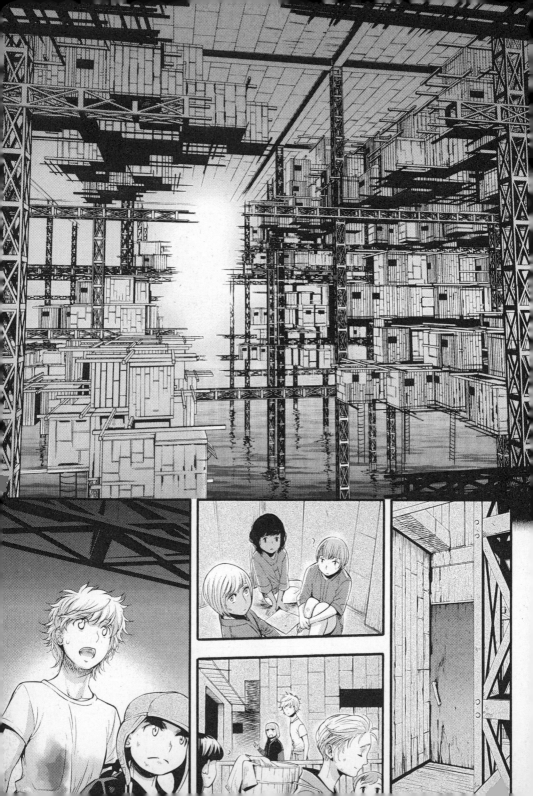

IT'S...THE ONLY GOOD THING LEFT IN THIS CRUMMY CITY, I GUESS.

IT'S... HARD TO DESCRIBE.

YOU HAVE TO SEE IT.

TAKE ME, TAKE ME!

TAKE ME!

OKAY.

ANYWAY, SHE WON'T STOP BUGGING ME UNTIL WE GO.

WHAT ARE YOU DOING?

CREAK

YOU'LL SEE.

TAKE ME!

TAKE ME!

WOW...

HEY, WAIT A SECOND, BEM.

THIS DOESN'T MAKE SENSE.

WHY WASN'T THIS DESTROYED LIKE EVERYTHING ELSE?

THE SKY ISN'T REAL. IT'S A DOME.

MY DAD TOLD ME IT'S MADE OF A SPECIAL GLASS THAT DOES SOMETHING TO LIGHT, LETS IT IN BUT NOT OUT.

LONG AGO, THERE WAS A WAR AND THE CHILDREN'S PARK WAS BOMBED, SO THEY MADE THIS NEW ONE INDOORS.

EVEN THE OUTER ONES COULDN'T FIND IT.

THANK GOD...

ALL IS NOT LOST.

RUSTLE

ELEPHANTS!!

HEY GUYS, COULD YOU EXPLAI—

DASH

THERE WAS A RUMOR THAT AN ALIEN PERSON ESCAPED FROM ERGENT SETH'S STARSHIP.

HE SENT YOU, DIDN'T HE?

NOW HE'S SENDING SPIES, IS THAT IT?

I'M NOT A SPY.

LIKE YOU WOULDN'T LIE TO ME IF YOU WERE.

SLAP

HER HAND NEVER MOVED—SHE SMACKED ME WITH HER MIND!

LET GO OF ME AND—

THANK YOU.

YOU'VE HELPED ME REMEMBER...

...THE WAY IT USED TO BE.

FINALLY...

...I HAVE A REAL CONNECTION TO MY FAMILY.

TO WHO I AM.

TO WHAT I WAS PUT IN THE UNIVERSE TO DO.

!!

!!

THUD

DANIEL?!

WHAT'S WRONG?

URGH...

...THE PAIN...

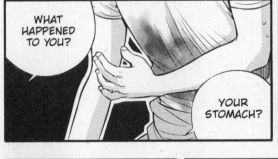

WHAT HAPPENED TO YOU?

YOUR STOMACH?

TELL ME, BEFORE YOU PASS OUT.

I WAS... SHOT...

...WITH...A 24/24 OPUS MAGNUM.

MUST HAVE USED A DELAYED FRAG ROUND.

TINY CHARGE INSIDE THE BULLET. CAN BE ACTIVATED AT A LATER DATE. EVEN BY REMOTE CONTROL.

DANIEL X

BOOM

...EXPLO-SION?

WHERE AM I....? AH, SURGERY...

CHAPTER 6

A SCREW-DRIVER? COME ON!

WELL, WHAT DO YOU KNOW?

I CAN'T BELIEVE IT.

YOU'RE ACTUALLY ALIVE.

WHAT HAP-PENED?

THE SMOKE?

I MANAGED TO GET THE BULLET OUT OF YOU, BUT IT BLEW UP...

...RIGHT WHEN I WAS TRYING TO TOSS IT OUT THE WINDOW.

HOW ARE YOU FEELING?

WELL...

...LIKE A MILLION BUCKS.

THANK YOU, UM...

I DIDN'T CATCH YOUR NAME, DOCTOR.

NO DOCTOR. JUST BLALEEN.

THANK YOU, EH, BLA-LEEN, FOR SAVING MY LIFE.

FOR... WHATEVER YOU DID HERE.

WAIT A SECOND.

YOU HAVEN'T SEEN MY WATCH, HAVE YOU?

I WAS WEARING IT A...

AH, DON'T MENTION IT.

OH, DEAR ME.

NO.

PLEASE, NO.

DANIEL!

LITTLE ONES...

...SAY HELLO TO YOUR GREAT-COUSIN DANIEL.

DANIEL X, TO BE PRECISE.

HE DOESN'T USE A FAMILY NAME BECAUSE HE DOESN'T HAVE A FAMILY.

UNTIL NOW, THAT IS.

I'M YOUR UNCLE KRAFFLEPROG, YOUR MOM'S BROTHER.

I'M YOUR COUSIN LYLAH.

TELL ME EVERY- THING.

WHO I AM.

WHO THE ALIEN HUNTERS ARE.

WHAT MY PARENTS WERE DOING ON EARTH.

WHERE—

WHOA, WHOA!

I'LL GIVE YOU THE SHORT VERSION, DANIEL.

LISTEN NOW.

MANY HUNDREDS OF YEARS AGO, OUR SPACE PROBES DISCOVERED EARTH.

WHAT AMAZED US WAS HOW SIMILAR OUR PLANETS WERE, IN TEMPERATURE, ATMOSPHERE, BODIES OF WATER.

IT WAS DISCOVERED THAT THE HUMAN HEART WAS ALSO SIMILAR TO THAT OF ALPARIANS, PHYSICALLY, AND IN OTHER WAYS AS WELL. IT WAS SUGGESTED THAT OUR RACES MIGHT HAVE DESCENDED FROM A SINGLE ANCESTOR.

UNFORTUNATELY, WE SOON LEARNED THE OUTER ONES HAD ALREADY DISCOVERED EARTH AND WERE WORKING TO COLONIZE AND TAKE IT OVER.

MY SON, GRAFF, MET AND FELL IN LOVE WITH YOUR MOTHER, ATRELDA, WHEN THEY WERE AT UNIVERSITY.

THEY BOTH HAD POWERS, DANIEL, TELEPATHY AND TRANSFORMING ABILITY.

THEY COULD, WELL, CREATE THINGS AT WILL.

IT'S RARE, BUT IT HAPPENS HERE.

DID YOU TELL HIM ABOUT HIS RATING?

THIS IS LIKE A MEMORY HOME MOVIE.

IT'S ONE OF OUR ABILITIES.

!!

THAT'S—!

WILLY!

EMMA!

DANA!

JOE!

WAIT A SECOND!

THAT'S JOE, WILLY, EMMA, AND DANA. MY FRIENDS!

YES, THEY WERE YOUR FRIENDS FROM PRE-SCHOOL.

MY, HOW YOU USED TO GET ON.

YOU FORMED A FRIENDSHIP BOND, CALLED A DRANG...

...THAT IS RARELY SEEN AMONG OUR PEOPLE. VERY POWERFUL, DANIEL. VERY SPECIAL.

BUT WHERE ARE THEY NOW? I HAVE TO SEE THEM IMMEDIATELY.

I KNOW
THINGS
LOOK
BAD NOW,
DANIEL.

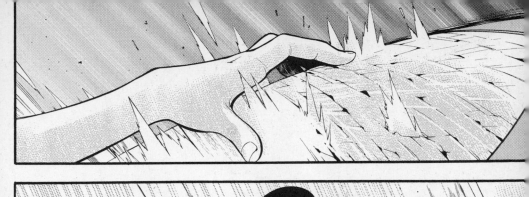

CRASH

WHAT THE—?!

PREPARE TO FIRE ON MY ORDER!

AND SUMMON MORE BACKUP.

I WANT A FULL SQUADRON OF BATTLE TANKS AND MISSILE DRONES!

GET ME A MILLION SQUADRONS!

ANYBODY MOVES...

...THEY'RE DEAD.

SAME GOES FOR YOU, SETH.

ON EARTH, THIS IS WHAT THEY CALL A MEXICAN STANDOFF.

YOU MOVE, YOU DIE.

I MOVE, I DIE.

I'LL TEACH YOU A LESSON.

IT WON'T TAKE LONG.

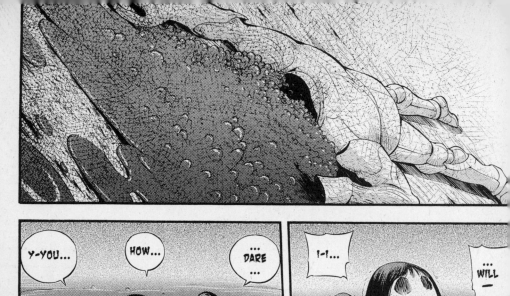

Y-YOU...

HOW...

...DARE...

I-I...

...WILL—

SWISH

THUD

DANIEL!!

YOU DID IT!!

YOU THERE.

M-ME?

YES, YOU.

WHAT'S YOUR NAME?

K...KROTH-GARK, SIR.

KROTH-GARK.

I HAVEN'T DECIDED IF I'M GOING TO LET YOU LIVE OR NOT.

WOULD YOU LIKE TO INFLUENCE MY DECISION?

YES, VERY MUCH.

THEN DO YOURSELF A BIG FAVOR AND LET THE KIDS FROM EARTH GO. ALL OF THEM.

YOU GOT IT, SIR.

RIGHT AWAY, RIGHT AWAY. YOU HEARD THE MAN!

......

UM... THANK YOU... AND...

...I FOUND THIS ON THE SHIP. I THOUGHT IT MIGHT BE IMPORTANT.

MY LAPTOP! THANK YOU!

23

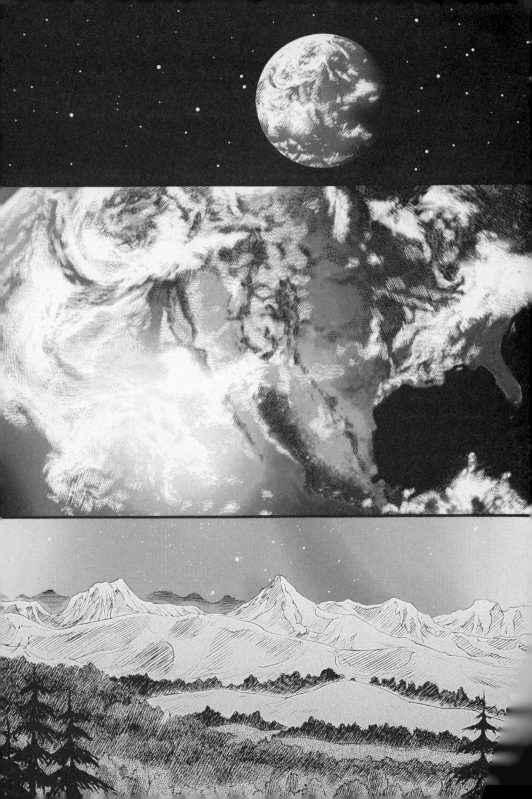

SO...

...WHY ARE WE...

...BACK ON EARTH AGAIN?!

IF WE'D STAYED ON ALPAR NOK...

...WE WOULD HAVE HAD A FEAST EVERY DAY!

......

I LOVE IT HERE.

IT'S A GREAT, GREAT PLANET.

THIS IS MY HOME.

BESIDES, I HAVE TO FINISH THE WORK MY PARENTS STARTED.

I CAN'T EVEN IMAGINE HOW I WOULD FEEL...

...IF SOMETHING HAPPENED TO EARTH WHILE I WAS GONE.

I'LL MISS MY GRAND-MA...

...BUT I'LL GET TO SEE HER AGAIN, I'M SURE.

DANIEL...

...NO MATTER WHAT YOU DECIDE TO DO...

...REMEM-BER THAT YOU'VE ALWAYS GOT US!

Read on to enjoy a preview of
MAXIMUM RIDE: THE MANGA
The hit adaptation of
author James Patterson's
bestselling novel series!
Volumes 1 to 3 available now!

JAMES PATTERSON
art by NaRae Lee

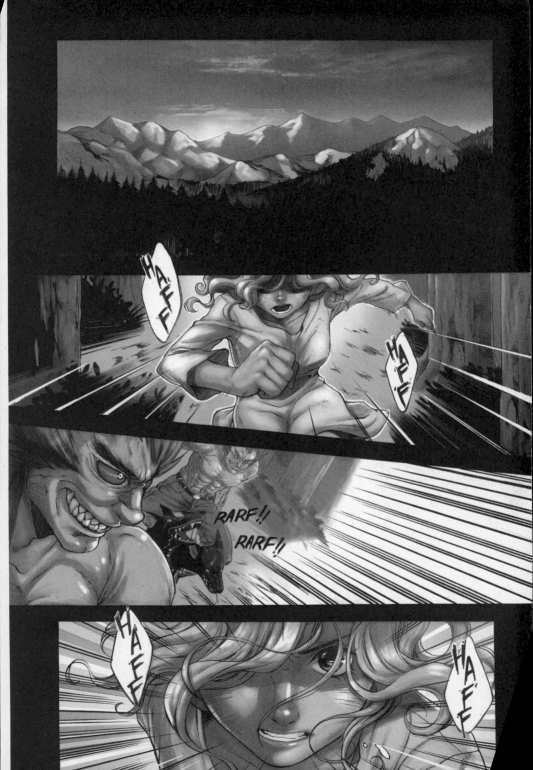

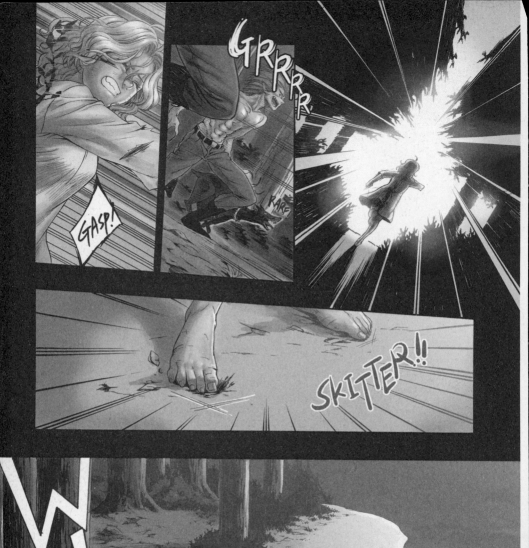

MAXIMUM
RIDE
CHAPTER 1

WHEN WE FIRST MOVED INTO THIS SECLUDED HOUSE...

...JEB BATCHELDER TOOK CARE OF US, LIKE A DAD.

GOOD MORNING, JEB.

TWO YEARS AGO, HE DISAPPEARED. WE ALL KNEW HE WAS DEAD, BUT WE DIDN'T TALK ABOUT IT.

AND NOW, AS THE OLDEST, I'M TRYING TO KEEP THINGS RUNNING IN HIS PLACE...AS BEST I CAN!

YAWN~

WHUMP!

ACK!

WOBBLE

WOBBLE

I'LL POUR JUICE.

WHO MOVED THE TABLE NEXT TO THE STAIRS?!

SORRY, IGGY.

THE STAIRCASE JUST LOOKED SO EMPTY.

DON'T FORGET I'M BLIND.

THEN PLEASE ACT LIKE YOU ARE.

FLOP

RUMMAGE RUMMAGE

UMM... WISH THE FOOD FAIRIES HAD COME...

FANG!! WILL YOU QUIT THAT?!

QUIT WHAT? BREATHING?

I'LL MAKE EGGS.

MAKE SOME NOISE WHEN YOU MOVE! YOU STARTLED ME!

WOBBLE

I DON'T WANT MAX TO BURN OUR LAST FRYING PAN.

Huh? Fang, when did you get up??

......

FINE. I'LL GO GET NUDGE AND ANGEL.

......

Look for MAXIMUM RIDE: THE MANGA in bookstores now!

1 NaRae Lee   **2** NaRae Lee   **3** NaRae Lee

GET YOUR MANGA FIX!!

Can't wait for the next volume of the *DANIEL X* or *MAXIMUM RIDE* manga to hit the bookstores? Now you can read the latest installments of your favorite manga in *YEN PLUS*, the monthly online magazine!

Just go to **www.yenpress.com** and hit the magazine tab to sign up for a monthly subscription, and you can read new chapters of *MAXIMUM RIDE*, *DANIEL X*, and more before adding the books to your collection!

Reading great manga online has never been easier!

DANIEL X: THE MANGA ①

JAMES PATTERSON
WITH MICHAEL LEDWIDGE
& SEUNGHUI KYE

Adaptation and Illustration: SeungHui Kye

Lettering: JuYoun Lee & Abigail Blackman

First published in the United States in 2010 by Yen Press, an imprint of Hachette Book Group, Inc.
First published in Great Britain in 2010 by Atom

DANIEL X, THE MANGA, Vol. 1 © 2010 by James Patterson

Illustrations © 2010 Hachette Book Group, Inc.

The moral right of the author has been asserted.

All characters and events in this publication, other than those clearly in the public domain, are fictitious and any resemblance to real persons, living or dead, is purely coincidental.

All rights reserved.
No part of this publication may be reproduced, stored in a retrieval system, or transmitted, in any form, or by any means, without the prior permission in writing of the publisher, nor be otherwise circulated in any form of binding or cover other than that in which it is published and without a similar condition including this condition being imposed on the subsequent purchaser.

A CIP catalogue record for this book is available from the British Library.

ISBN 978-1-907410-52-9

Printed in the United States of America

Atom
An imprint of Little, Brown Book Group
100 Victoria Embankment London EC4Y 0DY

An Hachette UK Company
www.hachette.co.uk

www.atombooks.net